DORA the EXPLORER™

LEARNING WORKBOOK

FIRST WORDS

BENDON™

Bendon Publishing International, Inc.
Ashland, OH 44805
www.bendonpub.com

star
la estrella

Trace the letters to write the word **star** below.

star

Find the two **stars** that are the same. Circle them.

1. 2. 3.
4.
5. 6.

flower
la flor

Trace the letters to write the word **flower** below.

flower

Finish drawing the picture of a **flower** for Dora and Boots.

book
el libro

Trace the letters to write the word **book** below.

Dora is reading a **book**. What is your favorite book?

Draw a picture of a character from your favorite **book**.

moon
la luna

Trace the letters to write the word **moon** below.

moon

Shhhh! Boots is napping on the **moon**.
Connect the dots to finish the picture.
Color the stars and sky.

Start

Finish

Review

Draw a line from each picture to the matching English and Spanish words.

book

el libro

moon

la luna

flower

la flor

star

la estrella

Review

Fill in the missing letter for each word. Write the entire word on the line below.

_ tar

_lower

_ook

_oon

apple
la manzana

Trace the letters to write the word **apple** below.

apple

Dora is holding an **apple**. Draw and color a tree full of **apples** so Dora can pick some more.

sun
el sol

Trace the letters to write the word **sun** below.

sun

Boots and Dora are sitting in the **sun**. Dora is wearing **sun**glasses.

rabbit
el conejo

Trace the letters to write the word **rabbit** below.

rabbit

Find and circle the two **rabbits** that are exactly the same.

1.

2.

3.

4.

5.

6.

Dora and Boots are hopping like the **rabbit**.

shoe
el zapato

Trace the letters to write the word **shoe** below.

shoe

Dora is wearing white **shoes**.

Draw lines between the **shoes** that match.

Review

Draw a line from each picture to the matching English and Spanish words.

rabbit   el zapato

shoe   el conejo

apple   la manzana

sun   el sol

Review

Fill in the missing letter for each word.
Write the entire word on the line below.

___pple

___un

___abbit

___hoe

bed
la cama

Trace the letters to write the word **bed** below.

Dora is napping in a **bed**. Draw a picture of what she might be dreaming about. Finish coloring the picture of the **bed**.

car
el carro

Trace the letters to write the word **car** below.

car

Boots, Tico and Dora are going for a ride in a **car**. Finish coloring the picture.

horse
el caballo

Trace the letters to write the word **horse** below.

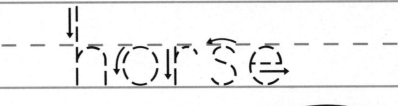

Dora and Boots are riding a **horse**. Color the picture.

hat
el sombrero

Trace the letters to write the word **hat** below.

hat

Dora is wearing a cowgirl **hat**. Look at the first hat in each box at the right. Color the matching hat in each row.

Review

Draw a line from each picture to the matching English and Spanish words.

car   el caballo

hat   el sombrero

bed   la cama

horse   el carro

Review

Fill in the missing letter for each word.
Write the entire word on the line below.

__ed

__orse

__ar

__at

family
la familia

Trace the letters to write the word **family** below.

family

Dora's **family** is having a party. Will you color the picture of Dora's **family**?

ball
la pelota

Trace the letters to write the word **ball** below.

ball

Dora is playing baseball. She caught the **ball** in her mitt.

Draw lines connecting the pictures that match.

train
el tren

Trace the letters to write the word **train** below.

train

Connect the dots to finish the picture of the **train**. Color the **train**.

Start

bike
la bicicleta

Trace the letters to write the word **bike** below.

bike

Dora is riding a **bike**.
Finish coloring the picture.

Review

Draw a line from each picture to the matching English and Spanish words.

train

el tren

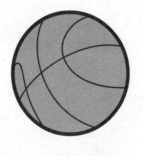

bike

la bicicleta

ball

la pelota

family

la familia

Review

Fill in the missing letter for each word.
Write the entire word on the line below.

__amily

__all

__rain

__ike

butterfly
la mariposa

Trace the letters to write the word **butterfly** below.

butterfly

Draw lines connecting the pictures of **butterflies** that match.

Dora is chasing **butterflies**. Finish coloring the picture.

present
el regalo

Trace the letters to write the word **present** below.

present

Connect the dots to finish the picture. Color the **presents**.

10 11 13 14
9 12 15
7 8
6
5
3 4
2
Start 1

bird
el pájaro

Trace the letters to write the word **bird** below.

bird

Color the **birds** that Boots and Dora are holding.
Draw some more **birds** in the sky.

balloon
el globo

Trace the letters to write the word **balloon** below.

balloon

Color the **balloons** Dora is holding.

Draw a line from each picture to the matching English and Spanish words.

bird   **el globo**

balloon   **el pájaro**

butterfly   **la mariposa**

present   **el regalo**

Review

Fill in the missing letter for each word. Write the entire word on the line below.

__utterfly

_____

- - - - - - - - - - - - - - - - - -

_____

__resent

_____

- - - - - - - - - - - - - - - - - -

_____

__ird

_____

- - - - - - - - - - - - - - - - - -

_____

__alloon

_____

- - - - - - - - - - - - - - - - - -

_____

Certificate of Completion

NAME

We did it!
¡Lo hicimos!